Windows PC
Buyer's Guide

Copyright 2016 by Mike Jessup

All rights reserved

Table of Contents

Introduction.

Decisions, decision. With so many computers on the market, how do you make the right choice? I've been working with computers and their users for almost two decades, buying, supporting and repairing computers for business and home use. There is no simple answer to the question, but one thing is certain, there is no one-size-fits-all computer. What is a great computer for you might be overkill for someone else. In order to find the best device for your needs you will have to consider what you are going to use it for. Is it for checking emails and playing solitaire? Or do you need financial software and photo editing capabilities? Whatever your specific needs, this book will help you determine the best computer and the best buy for *you*. Computers come in a wide range of prices, so buying more than you will ever use the computer for is wasting money, and resources. Once you know the specifications you can often find great deals by buying online or through special buys at local retailers.

*If you would like to learn more about working with Windows computers, visit us online at **www.itlight.net.***

Chapter 1. Buying a computer

It is rare these days to find anyone in the big box stores who know much about computers. Most of the young ones have enough experience to know some of the technical terms and they've probably helped their buddies and of course their parents with their computer problems. But it is highly unlikely that he or she has been tasked with keeping the computers running for a business or repairing them on a daily basis. Retailers also provide incentives for certain products over others, often the more expensive machines, which can significantly enhance the employee's paycheck. Is the associate steering you towards the computer that he likes or towards the one that will bring his bonus up in his next paycheck? You just might get someone who really knows what he's talking about, but will he know what your interests are? Will he take the time to ask you what you do with the computer and then, most importantly, will he have the real world experience to give you the straight talk about what will work best for you? I recently went shopping for a tablet PC to take on an out of town trip. I didn't have time to wait for online delivery so I went to several of the retailers in my mid-size home town. Only one of the sales associates was able to answer my simple questions, the others knew only what we both could read on the card next to the machine. So while we have lots of options for buying these days, getting reliable advice on making a purchase is hard to come by.

If you would rather not trust your dollars and the next few years with the computer to the kid at the store, here's some advice from a computer technician that has spent almost twenty years supporting computer users at home and at work. If you follow these guidelines, you will have a more stress-free life with your computer, whether at home or at work.

If you are thinking about a Mac, this book is not for you. They are preferred by those who do image editing, make audio files and write applications for Apple devices, but these are highly skilled tasks and most Apple users don't need any advice on what type of computer to get. A lot of what Apple users are after is how the computer looks and a certain 'cool' factor that is an integral part of the whole Apple brand. If you don't care as much about looks or know the names of any image editing programs, stick with a PC, or a Windows based computer. There are other operating systems out there like Linux and Chrome, but if you are into those you don't need to be reading this. Since there's really not much to tell about a Mac, other than you will be paying a lot more for one, the advice given here pertains to Windows based PCs.

BRANDS

I don't ever recommend one brand of computer over another. I've seen models of all types that are good and bad. Having worked with IBM, Dell, HP, Sony, Toshiba, Acer and a few others, as well as custom built machines I've decided that it's what inside the computer that counts, not who makes it. Many of the components inside the machine are the same across brands and many are made in the same factories in China. Ordering a certain model does not guarantee that the same components will be inside; I've seen instances of a hundred computers, the same model, all purchased at the same time with different components when opened up. And I've heard so many techs say good and bad things about every single brand that there really is not a consensus on one being consistently better than another one. One technician will hate a certain model and another one will prefer it over all others. A lot of times these techs are trying to support computers that are not designed for the functions they are being asked to perform. When that happens, you are asking for trouble and I can assure you that your computer will make you miserable. There is very little more frustrating than a computer that does not perform properly. This is why it is so important to buy a machine that has the proper components to perform the functions you are asking it to complete. Fortunately, it's not rocket science.

Specs

The two most important factors that will affect the performance of your computer are the **processor** and the amount of random access memory, or **RAM.**

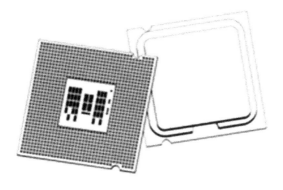

Bottom and top view of processor

These two factors alone will have the most effect on the performance of your computer. The processor is the brain of the computer. It does all of the mathematical calculations, all the sorting of bits and bytes, zeros and ones, that complete the tasks. I know this is a difficult concept to understand, how just ones and zeros can translate into computer instructions, but it isn't necessary to understand how it works in order to know that the processor is one of the most important components of your computer. In the US, there are two major brands of processors available in consumer PC's, **Intel** and **AMD**. Historically, the Intel processor was used in business class computers while the AMD was preferred by gamers. These days the lines are more blurred when it comes to which processor will perform better in either category. Except in certain circumstances described later on, either processor is fine for the average user. Let's take a quick overview of both types.

Here is where 'geek-speak' makes it very difficult to discuss which processor to buy. And while it's easy to get bogged down in all of the naming schemes, generally, the ***Intel Quad Core processor is the high end of the market***. Xeons sit at the top of the list but these are usually sold in server machines and high end workstations. The Xeon level of processor is capable of handling many times the commands needed by a single user's computer, whether for home or business use. A step down from the Xeons are the quad core processors, the i7, i5 and i3 generally found in desktops and laptops at the high end of the spectrum. Next you have the dual cores, the Pentiums and lastly the Celeron bringing up the lower cost, lower end of the spectrum. The speed, expressed in gigahertz (GHz) is not always a clear indication of the performance of the machine, but it is important to pay attention to. If you buy a processor at 1.8 GHz it will be slow, especially compared to a 3.0 GHz machine. I would recommend as close to 3.0 GHz as you can get when purchasing a new computer. Of course, the faster the processor, usually, the more expensive the computer. Try to get at least around 2.5 GHz if your budget allows for it. Computers with Celerons are typically priced considerably less than those with Pentiums. If you don't do any video or graphics work on your computer the Celeron will work just fine, but it will not be as fast as the dual core, Pentium or quad core processors. Celerons are stable work horses though and if you don't need the speed, then they are perfectly acceptable. If all you use the computer for is checking email, playing solitaire and doing a few Google searches a Celeron will work just fine. If you are impatient or like to run multiple programs, do a lot of online work or if you run any kind of financial software, try to get the higher end processor, at least a dual core. The quad cores are good, but most users can get by with dual core processors provided they have enough RAM. For business use a dual core, at least, with speed of 3.0 Ghz is recommended.

The other big player in the processor wars is **AMD**, maker of the Athlon processor. These are traditionally the top picks for gamers so if the new computer is for a teenager who is into video games in a big way, you will want to consider the Athlon processor. These also work fine for everyday computing and can be a good value with plenty of power for most user programs. However, if you are using it for databases and especially for any accounting software like Quickbooks, stick with the higher end Intel Pentium products for your processor.

Once you decide on a processor the other big piece of the puzzle is getting as much random access memory (**RAM**) as you can afford, at least 2 Gigs of RAM, and preferably 3 or 4 gigs (gigs is how to say gigabytes, or GB).

Four 'sticks' of RAM

Think of RAM as the amount of energy your computer has to do its job. In tech school they used to compare the amount of RAM to the size of your workspace, but I prefer to think of it as energy. You can have a blazing fast processor but without enough RAM the machine will lag and choke on the commands you give it. Increasing memory has a remarkable affect on performance. Four gigs of RAM these days are ideal and some machines have the option to expand up to 8 gigs or more if you want to. Be careful here though – unless you have a 64-bit operating system the computer will not be able to make use of more than 4 GB of RAM. It's more complicated than this booklet will go into, but all you really need to know is that the 64-bit operating system can use more RAM, (and is therefore potentially faster) and the 32-bit system will only be able to access 4 GB, so don't pay for more than that in a 32-bit system. You are wasting your money if you do. At any rate, more than 4 GB might be more than the average user will need unless you are using some heavy duty programs, gaming or doing video and graphics work. So a good average is two to four gigs of

RAM. Memory these days is not an expensive upgrade to a computer and will greatly affect its performance. Be sure to keep in mind that if you are getting a slower processor you can make up for that to a certain extent by increasing the RAM. So a computer with a Celeron processor and 8 gigs of RAM may work as well as a Dual Core processor with only 2 gigs of RAM, making sure that your operating system is 64-bit capable with the higher amount of memory.

In summary, for home users who only want a computer for occasional use for email, shopping, and basic programs like Word, Excel and Microsoft games, a low end processor rated at 2.5 Ghz with 2 GB of RAM will work fine. For more advanced users who are online most of the time and who may use more complex programs, upgrade to dual core with a processor speed closer to 3.0 Ghz and the RAM to 4 GB. Even more complex programs like image editing and some financial software would benefit from faster, multiple core processors and more RAM, remembering to choose a 64-bit operating system if trying to use more than 4 GB of RAM

Now is a good time for a discussion about the difference between memory and storage. A hard drive (storage) is where the operating system, your programs, and all of your data (these are documents you create, pictures you store, or anything you download) is stored.

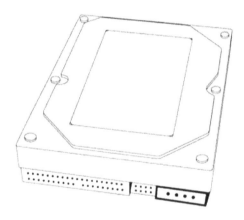

Old style PATA hard drive

When you turn off the computer all of this information remains safely written on the hard drive. When you turn on the computer, the processor loads the operating system and any programs you have set to start, into RAM, the memory. Memory has nothing to do with storage, it's very confusing but the technical gurus who invented these terms did not think about communicating them to the average person. When people say they need to delete files because their memory is full, this is a misunderstanding of how the computer works. A memory full error means you have too many programs open at one time or that in general the computer does not have enough 'energy', as explained above, to complete the commands you have given it. Deleting documents will have no effect on the memory. Closing down programs that are not in use will have a significant effect on memory. So the hard drive, storage, controls how much 'stuff' you can store on your computer. If you have lots of pictures, music or video, then you will need a larger hard drive, at least 500 GB or 1T (terabyte, or 1000 gigabytes). If you don't have lots of pictures, videos or music, you can get by with a smaller hard drive and save some money on your computer purchase. A 160 GB hard drive is more than you will ever fill up if you are storing the odd picture and word documents so there is no need to pay for the higher capacity hard drive. Most new computers sold today will come with a newer SATA hard drive (serial ATA, as opposed to parallel ATA). The SATAs allow for faster data transfer than the older style. The older style hard drives are still out there so it's important to know which type you are buying. Another thing to think about is how important your information is. All hard drives fail eventually, even if it doesn't happen until years down the road. SATA hard drives are much more difficult and expensive to recover data from if they do fail. The older PATA drives, while still expensive to recover data from, are in most cases 99% effective and cost much less than SATA drive data recovery. In either case backing up your information is necessary to avoid costly data recovery expenses in case of a hard drive failure.

A good quality **video card** is a must if you're gaming, but otherwise don't worry about it, just take what comes standard on the machine. The newer operating systems recommend a graphics card with onboard RAM. These are higher end cards than what you are likely to find in older machines. Gamers will want a high quality video card and these can be quite expensive, in some cases several hundred dollars. Serious gamers will build their own machine and purchase the video card separately. You must be very careful about reading the specs for these cards. Some require a larger than normal power supply to run them, and will not fit in small form factor machines, which are the most common computers sold these days. If you do a lot of image editing you will need to look more closely at the specs for the built in graphics card and follow the recommendations from the program developer. For normal computer use the video card will not matter, unless you want connections for television, and in that case you are looking at spending more money for upgraded graphics, processor and RAM. I like to keep the computer and television separate but if you want those connections look at the specs recommended by your television manufacturer. Newer televisions have internet capabilities built in and devices like the Roku and Xbox allow you to view content from the internet on your TV screen without hooking up the computer.

TYPE

Deciding which type of computer and by that I refer to laptop, desktop or tablet will depend on what you need to use it for. Let me give some general information on how to decide this.

The desktop computer is the least expensive to purchase, the least expensive to have worked on and the most powerful computer you can buy. If you don't need to take your computer with you, it will always be better off in the long run purchasing a desktop. Remember that the monitor is sold separately and that when replacing a desktop you can use the current monitor with the new computer. Desktops are less expensive because everything does not have to be compact as well as lightweight to fit inside the smaller form of a laptop. Also, repairing a desktop is almost always much less expensive because parts are usually readily available and easy to replace. In addition, if a built in part such as the video card or network adaptor fail on a desktop, you can easily purchase a replacement part that will fit in one of the expansion slots (see drawing below). This means you do not have to replace the whole system board, which is expensive both   for   parts   and   labor.

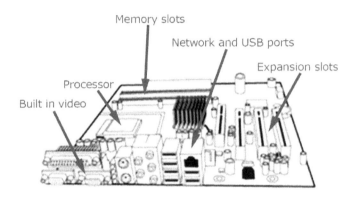

Desktop system board

Another thing to consider is whether or not you plan on installing high end image editing or financial programs. If you do then you will be better off with a desktop. Here I would suggest buying a standard desktop as opposed to small form factor as this will give you the opportunity to upgrade the graphics adaptor as well as the power supply to handle the higher quality hardware. Small form factors computers are designed to fit either under the desk or to turn on their side and put underneath a flat screen monitor. They measure about 12 – 14 inches in length and are about 4 – 5 inches wide and are fine for average use. Higher end equipment will not physically fit inside these computers because the chassis is too small even if they have the required adaptors. For those whose computer needs are average, with some emails, Microsoft Office and web surfing, a small form factor will be the best buy, take up less space either under the desk or on the desk with the monitor placed on top. For more advanced programs and upgraded graphics a standard desktop is the better choice.

Laptops are more expensive than desktops for the reasons listed above and because they are much more expensive to work on. This is because compared to a desktop where the side slips off without using any tools and most everything is readily accessible, with a laptop you need to take the whole thing apart to get to most of the components. The parts are more expensive as well so there's no getting around the fact that you will be paying more for the portability. In contrast to the desktop, when any of the built in components like the video card goes out on a laptop, the whole system board must be replaced; there are no expansion slots on a laptop. While higher end programs will run on a laptop provided you have a robust processor and plenty of RAM, I still recommend using a desktop for those programs if at all possible. Also as part of your decision making process, keep in mind that many laptops have a smaller keyboard, and a smaller screen. This means that if you are older and get eyestrain from looking at the computer all day, you'll need to purchase a larger monitor to go with the laptop. And unless you also purchase a stand for it you will be looking off to the side so that you can keep your keyboard in front of you. That's how I usually use my laptop, which I do take to client's sites regularly, and it works fine but takes some getting used to. Also be aware of the fact that most laptops don't have the full keyboard layout. What's usually missing is the numbers keypad, although some wide screen laptops do incorporate them. The full keyboard laptops are heavy though so if you are going to be carrying it often keep that in mind. I would try to steer clear of having a docking station with mouse and keyboard. A wireless mouse is good to have but get used to using the native laptop keyboard. The worst part about having a laptop is that you have to pack it all up and put it in a case. The fewer components you have to carry around with you, the better your experience will be. Most people adjust to it fine after a few weeks.

Tablets are the newest member of the computer family and there are many options to choose from. While most of these are not technically considered as Windows computers some do run the Windows operating system. Small and lightweight, they are good for internet access and emails when away from the desktop computer, or when you don't want to carry the laptop. Smaller tablets allow for touch typing directly on the screen, the same type of keyboard on a smartphone but a few models have keyboards which can be detached when not in use. If you type a lot, other than just a few lines here and there, you may want to consider a tablet with a keyboard. Otherwise the smaller ones are fine for light use. They are great for photos, checking email and quick internet viewing, but the screen is small compared to a full size computer or laptop and their functionality is a lot less than a laptop's. Most tablet users that I've come across have a desktop or laptop at home and use the tablet for a quick check of their email when out of the house.

Some computer users are attracted to the style of the all-in-one computer which has all of the components behind the monitor. These are more expensive than desktops and are also very expensive to work. Just like laptops these must be taken completely apart to fix anything, parts are expensive and there are no expansion slots.

The techies are all saying that the desktop is dead, but I suspect it will be around for a while simply because it's so versatile. Until we reach the age of disposable computers, the desktop is still the best value on the market.

Other components

As for other components in your laptop or desktop, do **get a DVD drive** in your computer. I see some of the new ones coming out with no optical drive at all (that's a DVD or CD drive). If you can get a DVD that writes CDs that would be the best option. Copying files to CD is still a fairly common practice and a good backup solution. Also, most software is installed via CD or DVD and the new trend is to have the software downloaded from the internet is fine, unless you find yourself with a computer problem and no way to reach the internet, which is often the case when things go wrong.

Your new computer should come with **plenty of USB ports**. The USB port is the best invention since the computer itself. I thank the guy who came up with it every time I use one because I remember how hard it used to be to install printers without it, not to mention the glory of having USB storage devices which have to be the quickest and easiest way to back up your data or move files from one computer to another. Get at least six USB ports on the machine if possible, although laptops generally come with less. Your mouse, keyboard and printer will take up two or three right off the bat, so if you only get four USB ports you will most likely be unplugging something to plug in something else.

All the other stuff is strictly up to your personal preference. After I bought my last laptop I found that I used the SD port quite often to transfer pictures from my digital camera to the computer, but it wasn't something that I couldn't do without. I already had another way to transfer the pictures, so it's nice but not necessary. You will want to consider whether or not to include ports for attaching your computer to your television. All I can say is that linking the computer and the television once and for all is on its' way so if you want to head in that direction, get those features as well. It complicates things and there are other devices you can use to watch internet video and movies on your television. I prefer keeping them separate, but if you want those features they are available in some configurations.

Now a word about the operating system. The fear of having to learn a new OS is probably the biggest factor holding people back when it comes to buying a new computer. For computers with Windows 8 installed the transitions is difficult, even for expert users. As of this writing Microsoft is offering free upgrades to Windows 10 for Windows 7 and Windows 8 users. If you can get a computer with Windows 7, it is an excellent operating system and will be in use for several years simply because so many businesses are using it right now that Microsoft will have to continue support for it. However, I would immediately upgrade any Windows 8 operating system to Windows 10 without even bothering trying to use Windows 8 first. Windows 8 was a dud,

Microsoft has a poor operating system once in a while, and 8 is one of them. Windows XP was a very good operating system and if you still have it on your old machine you will be fine if your new computer has Windows 7 or Windows 10. Windows 7 is very much like Windows XP, but it is only available with online purchases, usually with a refurbished machine. If you are still running Windows XP and upgrade to Windows 8 you may have a hard time using the computer, Windows 8 is something very different from previous operating systems. The hardest thing to deal with is that there's no Start button. That's right, the Start button, which is how you get to almost everything on the computer in a Windows-based system, is gone! Instead, there are tiles on the computer screen that take you to the various items that used to be in your start menu. Windows 8 was designed for touch screen computing and it seems that Microsoft jumped the gun on how quickly everyone would be ditching their home computers in favor of smart phones and tablets. The problem with touch screens is that it is still, and will be for a long time, so much easier to type on a keyboard than on a screen. But Microsoft realized it's mistake and the upgrade to Windows 8, which is Windows 8.1, did reinstall the start button, although it still has the tiles available for use as well. Windows 10 is kind of mixture of both Windows 7 and Windows 8. One thing Microsoft does do is listen to it's customers. It has hundreds of millions of them world wide so it's a good thing. Before purchasing a new computer I would recommend going into an office supply store or a big box store and looking at the different operating systems available even if you are going to order online. That way you will be familiar with how the new operating system will look. Now that Windows 8 is easily upgraded to Windows 10, Windows XP users should have no problem transitioning to the new operating system.

You should also be aware that all support for Windows XP is ended in April 2014. What this means is that no new updates to the operating system, no new drivers or programs will be written or supported for machines running on Windows XP. Also keep in mind that XP machines will no longer meet security standards after spring of 2014. While XP is still a good operating system, the lack of support for it and the security issues are both good reasons to upgrade.

Purchasing

Generally speaking, you will get a better price on a computer when buying online than in a retail store. It's very hard to compare exactly because the specs are a little different for each computer. I would recommend checking out some of the sales at the big box electronics stores and then go online and look for a similar computer and see what the difference in price is. Look on the same retailer's site for other deals that may not be available in the stores. Be sure to compare the processor type and speed, the amount of RAM and the size of the hard drive. You will find a lot more options when searching online. Most retailers only have a few computers for sale in the store and there a hundreds if not thousands to choose from on the internet. If you are more comfortable buying from a store rather than online that's fine too. Be sure to check your specs just as you would when searching online.

There are a couple of things to look at when buying a computer online. First is the warranty. In the old days a standard warranty on a new computer was three years with an option to extend up to five years. Now a one year warranty is standard and many come with only 30 to 90 days. I would not purchase a computer with less than a one year warranty, period even though I can easily repair the computer myself. To me it indicates a seller who is not willing to stand behind his product. Purchasing an extended warranty is optional. I never extend them but am able to work on the computer myself for usually less than what the extension would cost. Sometimes extending the warranty is more than the cost of a new computer so be sure to check out the details before buying.

Second, what types of reviews are showing for the model you are interested in purchasing? If there are only a few reviews and most of them are not favorable, don't purchase. I look for a good volume of reviews and then read several of them to see if most users are happy with their product. One or two unhappy computer users out of a few dozen does not scare me away. Some computer users are never happy no matter what machine they have. If most of the reviews are positive then I take that as a sign that in general it's a good machine

Thirdly, make sure the seller allows returns. Not that you will want to return the machine but it's good to know that if you just end up not liking it and want to return it for another one, you can do so. Sometimes you will have to pay shipping charges for the return but it might be worth it in the long run. By the way, I always ship computers FedEX and so do most sellers.

One place to get good deals on computers is on eBay, but you have to be careful with purchasing this way. I would not buy a computer from an individual but there are several companies selling refurbished equipment through eBay and some of them are very good. Look at their overall approval rating and choose one of at least 98%. Check the number of units sold as another indicator that this is not someone looking to unload some equipment. If they show thousands of computers sold and a high satisfaction rating then they will probably be a good source for refurbished computers. Often these computers are turned back in after a corporate lease expires or a company goes out of business. If it's a good company they will be bench tested and repaired if needed before being sold. I've worked for companies who regularly buy equipment this way and it can save hundreds of dollars on the price of a computer. Usually there will be some minor signs of wear on the machine but if you don't mind a scuff or a scratch I can recommend this as a good way to purchase computers.

Chapter 2. Setting up the computer.

Once you decide on which computer best fits your needs and make your purchase, you'll need to set it up for the first time. Plugging in all the wires is easy: there's really no way to mess it up, just make sure you have them all plugged in. The operating system will prompt you for the language and country when it starts up. Then you will need to select the time zone, which is sometimes correct and sometimes not. Be sure to check the box that checks for Daylight Savings Time. The next item will be setting up a user account and a password. You can name the user account anything you like. If more than one person uses the computer just make the user account one of the person's names; you can add another account later on.

A note about passwords. Put a password on your machine. Don't make it something so obvious that a stranger can guess it. The most common passwords are password, or password1, or the user name, which is spelled out right there on the screen, or the username1. Make it something a stranger would have no reason to know, like your pet's name unless you have it plastered all over the room where someone can see it, or a combination of parts of a couple of names. The most secure passwords have symbols and numbers mixed in with letters, both upper case and lower case and are not a complete word that you would find in a dictionary. **But almost any password is better than no password at all**. What most people don't realize until it's too late is, that if you don't put a password on your computer and someone steals it, they can plug it in, turn it on and get access to your email, your documents and in a lot of cases, banking information and accounts, if you have the browser remember your passwords for you. That's pretty scary, and you can prevent most thieves from doing this simply by using a good password. It's possible to crack passwords with software but most thieves will not have the ability to do it. So what usually happens is they will have to re-install the operating system, which will write over all the files on the computer. Just by putting a password on the user account you have prevented them from getting access to the information on your computer, which these days is more and more confidential. We tend to use our computers for everything, from taxes, to pictures, to medical information. The password doesn't need to be so hard that you can't remember it. I can't tell you the number of times I've seen a password on a sticky noted attached to a monitor. Needless to say that defeats the purpose. If you have to write it down, put it somewhere away from the computer. But do put a password on your user account and make it something that you can easily remember but that no one else could guess.

Chapter 3. Getting to the internet.

Setting up your internet connection is the first thing most people do after their computer is up and running. Whether you have DSL from the phone company or broadband from your cable provider the set up works the same way. What you want to try to avoid is having to call either the telephone company or the cable company to help you, simply because the wait times can be enormous. I've never known anyone who enjoyed that process. The only thing that makes it difficult at all is that the terms we use to describe the various components often get confused. So here it is, the straight scoop. Your telephone line or your cable wire will connect from the wall to a device that is usually owned or provided by the internet carrier. This we will call a modem, since it modulates (and demodulates) the signal from whatever it is coming through the outside wires as, to digital signals your computer can read. If you have only one computer in your home you can connect directly to this device, but it is preferable to place a broadband router between the modem and your computer, especially if you have more than one internet device in your home. This also provides another level of security from the outside world (highly recommended these days). So assuming that you have a modem, a router and a computer here's the setup procedure. Connect the modem to the outside source, either the telephone line or the cable wire, and power up. Always start the modem first. It takes some time for all of the lights to come on so be patient until they do. If you see any lights that are yellow or some do not come on you will have to call your provider, who will tell you to unplug the device, let it sit for a few minutes and then plug it back in (this is the same thing as rebooting your computer), so try that first before you call them. Now that the modem is up and running, plug your router into the modem, plug the computer into the router, and plug in the power to the outlet. If you have software that came with the router follow the set up procedure. Most times if everything is working properly, the computer will connect and go right out to the internet. However, if you have wireless on your router, you need to set up some kind of password or access key so that your neighbors can't connect to your network without your permission. This will involve going into the router settings and will differ depending on what router you use. It is not a good practice to leave your wireless network unsecured, so get help with this step if you need it. Basically all that is involved is putting a password, or key on the router and then putting that same password or key into the computer or other wireless device when it tries to connect. You only have to do it one time, not every time you connect. Be careful about telling the wireless connection setup to connect automatically any time the wireless network is available. That's fine for home but not always ok for other connections. Remember, when you connect to a network, at least some of your data is visible to others on that network.

The first thing to do after you get connected to the internet is to go to Windows update and let any updates for the operating system install. This may take a few reboots to finish. Always keep trying to update until the update service tells you there are no more important updates for your computer. The reason this takes more than one time is that some updates require previous versions before they can install: they are built on an earlier update. So don't think that once you've clicked on install updates once you are through with that process. Keep going back until there are no more.

Chapter 4. Installing software.

Once you get the operating system up and running, and connect to the internet you will need to install your programs, like Microsoft Office, or Quickbooks. Sometimes your new computer will have office software installed on it already, but usually it does not. You will need to install any programs that you use separately after you get the computer booted up. Microsoft Office does not come standard on new computers, so make sure you have the installation CDs for your Office Suite, and the key code so you can re-install it. Otherwise you're looking at purchasing another version of Office, and the new ones have a steep learning curve compared to the older versions. These days you can purchase your software online but it's preferable to have it on CD. That way if you get a virus and have to wipe your hard drive, you can install the software much more easily than if you have to call Microsoft and explain to them what happened. In some cases you can download the software again from the Microsoft website, but only if you have a valid key code that goes with it. Either way, make sure you keep all of the information regarding the purchase, and especially the product key, which is a long string of capital letters and numbers with dashes between them. Usually it is printed on the back of the CD casing or on the envelope housing the casing, or in the case of downloaded software, in an email sent to you after payment. Just use the defaults for setup.

Take off programs you aren't likely to use. New computers these days come with lots of freebie trial software that you most likely won't ever use. Take these programs off and your machine will run much faster from the beginning. The fewer icons you have in your system tray, which is the bar right next to the time at the bottom right corner of your screen, the faster your computer will run. I recently went to install a router for a computer whose owner had shut it down for the install, which wasn't necessary anyway. The machine took over fifteen minutes to boot, during which time I could not do anything but sit and look out the window. When it finally finished there were over a dozen items in the system tray, each one of which had to load automatically when the computer started. A few programs, which if they are installed its best to leave them, are Adobe Reader, which you will need to read PDF files, and Flash player, which you most likely won't see listed as a program since it runs mostly in the browser. If these are installed, leave them and if they are not, go to the Adobe website, which is Adobe.com, and get these free downloads. Be careful because there are lots of sites which try to disguise themselves as Adobe and add other things to your computer during the download. Just make sure you go to the Adobe.com site and not some look alike. I've noticed that when searching for the Adobe reader in the Ask browser, you get a lot of things, but not the real site, which is a good reason not to use Ask or anything other than Google when searching. It is by far the best search engine out there and does not give phony results like those I've found on Yahoo and Ask. If you aren't careful those search engines can get you into a lot of trouble.

Chapter 5. Setting up your email

Basically, there are two ways to access your email. One is to use an email client such as Outlook or Thunderbird to download your email to the computer you are using. The other is to go to the hosting site and view it online. There are advantages to each method as well as disadvantages. Outlook, which is probably the most popular email client, is a robust program, one of the most complex programs you will ever use on your computer. Thunderbird, a free download from Mozilla, is also an email client but does not have all of the functions of Outlook. If you use Outlook, you need to be aware that you are storing your email on your computer and that if it crashes you may lose the emails stored there, unless you are lucky and have a backup. However, backups of documents do not include email files by default, so you have another step in backing up to make sure that you include your email file. Outlook can be purchased separately or as part of a Microsoft Office package, which will usually always include

Word and Excel, and possibly Access, depending on which version you opt for. If you don't need a high-end email client, Thunderbird by Mozilla is free and has a scaled down version of the Outlook calendar called Lightning, which can be downloaded as an add-on. Thunderbird is an excellent program, and is very easy to download and install. It will do the configuration for you in most cases, without having to enter more than your email address and password.

Depending on where your email is hosted, you may want to view it online and not set up an email client at all. All of the Internet service providers have an email login on their web pages. It just means that there's an extra step to get to the page. There's also usually a limit on how many emails you can store in the mailbox online, so if you never delete anything (not a good idea!) you will constantly be running up against the limit and even have email blocked once you reach your quota; any messages delivered to a full mailbox will be returned to the sender. Many people access their email this way and it works fine. I prefer to use Thunderbird because it is so simple, but I don't use any fancy editing in my emails or make use of the calendar or contacts functions.

Chapter 6. Transferring your data

One of the questions I am asked all the time is, if programs (the most common are Microsoft Word, Excel, and Outlook) will transfer from an old computer to a new one. The simple answer is no. Back in the beginning of Windows operating systems, most programs were easy to copy and install on a new computer, but those days are long gone. Unless you have the installation files, usually on CD, you cannot install programs on your new computer. It's a good idea to keep the original disks in an envelope or folder for safe keeping. Otherwise you will need to purchase a new copy of the program.

But everything else, your documents, pictures, music, videos – all of the personal information, that is, information created by you, by someone who sent it to you, is transferrable. The easiest way to do this is to make a backup of your 'stuff' (a highly technical term) to a removable hard drive or USB thumb drive. These are available at any electronics store.

Something to think about here is that if you can get a USB drive large enough to hold all of your stuff, you can put it in your purse or attach it to your key ring so that it goes with you when you leave your computer. That way, if disaster strikes in the form of fire, weather event, or theft, you have a copy of the information on your computer. As long as you remember to do your backup frequently....which reminds me, I need to backup my files. Now where did I put that USB drive?.....

The only hard thing about doing a backup is finding the files you need to store. Use the copy and paste feature available in all Windows computers. For example, find your Documents folder, right click and select copy, then click on your USB drive in Windows Explorer to open it, put your cursor in a blank area of the file space, right click and select paste. This will place a copy of the Documents folder on the USB drive. It's a good idea, especially until you get the hang of it, close everything out and then browse to the USB drive to make sure your copied files are there. Open one or two of them up just to be on the safe side. The process for all of your files is the same: navigate to the file you want to copy, right click, select copy, then go the destination folder (where you are going to put a copy of it for safe keeping) right click, select paste. Do this with your pictures, videos, favorites and anything you may have stored on your desktop. Try to do a backup at least once a month and if you suspect your computer has a problem of any kind. Recently I had an error message when trying to log on and realized that my data had not been backed up since I had created several new documents and made important changes to a few others. As soon as I was able to get the computer working I did my backup, so now if it is failing (it was probably caused by an unwanted program which I deleted) I have everything I need from it.

In conclusion, all computers fail in the end and while it's possible to repair most of them, at some point it becomes more economical to purchase a new machine, especially as the age of your computer increases.

*If you would like to learn more about Windows computers, visit us online at **www.itlight.net***

Troubleshooting Tips

There really is an art to it, and every tech practices his or her art in a different way. My way is a common sense approach.

> *"How many computer helpdesk technicians does it take to change a light bulb?*
> *It only takes one, but they don't actually change the bulb, they just tell you to turn it off and then turn it back on again."*

When the computer is doing strange things or 'acting up' the first thing to try, before you call anyone or do anything else, is to shut the computer down, wait two minutes, and then power the computer back up. The best explanation I have ever heard for why this is a necessary step is this. We all know that computers run on a binary language, which simply means that their instructions are made up of series of zeros and ones, kind of like Morse code with its series of dots and dashes. These instructions that the computer uses to complete its tasks are loaded from the hard drive each time the computer boots up; that is it gets a complete copy of code from storage.

Over time, some of the zeros get mistaken for ones and vice versa, and so the set of instructions running the computer becomes corrupt. The solution is to power down, which dumps the current batch of instruction files into the trash can, and when you power up again, it loads a fresh, uncorrupted set of instructions into the computer's memory. This tip works for many digital devices, including cell phones and networking equipment. Also, certain tasks are completed at boot up which are not normally done at any other time. Try it before you call for tech support next time.

When choosing an email name, don't make it anything readable. By making your user name, which is the part before the '@' symbol, unreadable, it cuts down dramatically on the amount of spam that you receive in your mailbox. This is especially true if your email is hosted by one of the big internet service providers (ATT, Charter, etc.) Spammers use computer generated names to send out their spams, running through 'common name' lists to create hundreds of thousands of potential email addresses. When you spell out your name, johndoe@yourdomain.com, it's easy for the dictionary to put ordinary first and last names together and send out spam. Once it finds a deliverable email address, it often sells that address to other mail lists. Making your email less decipherable to a computer spam program will help enormously in cutting down on unwanted junk email.

For your own protection, **set up a password protected screen saver** on your computer, especially if you use the device for any type of financial programs like Quick Books or do your taxes with Turbo Tax. If your computer ever gets stolen not only will you lose the computer, but all of your information, including your banking and tax information, will be visible to whoever takes your computer if it is not password protected. With a password, it becomes much more difficult to get that information. Most times computers are not sold for the information they contain but for their re-sale value: the existing data will be erased and the operating system will be re-installed for sale as a 'new' computer.

Use a different browser. A browser is a computer program designed for using the internet – it 'browses' web pages. All Windows computers come with Internet Explorer (Microsoft has gotten into some trouble for this in the past), but you can install and use a variety of other browsers on any Windows machine. Mozilla's Firefox is an excellent browser, as is Google's Chrome. Be sure when doing the installation to check the box 'use as my default browser, or else Internet Explorer will open any time you click on a link from email.

Beware when installing programs downloaded from the internet, such as the browsers listed above, of unwanted add-ons, like trial versions of anti-virus software packages. Make sure you work through the installation slowly and uncheck any boxes that are signing you up for additional programs. You can always go back and add those later if you decide you want them.

Only one anti-virus program at a time, please. Anti-virus software programs typically do not play well together, so don't try to install McAfee and Norton AV on the same machine. One will disable the other anyway, so there's no point really. It doesn't give you double protection and can cause a lot of headaches down the road. Some free anti virus programs will not play well with your other installed programs, for instance, it may block your email as a means of protecting the computer. All of the big name anti-virus packages are priced about the same so take your pick. It is important to remember that your anti-virus is only as good as your last update. It is not possible at this time, to anticipate all of the new viruses that come out during a year, so the anti-virus updates include the latest 'virus definitions', which are specific to each virus. Remember that all anti-virus programs have two parts, the installation of the software and the updates. It is best to set up automatic updates and scans on your computer and to check it once in a while and make sure it is running.

Malware protection is as important, if not more so, than virus prevention. There are several good anti-malware products out there, particularly Spybot Search and Destroy, and Malware Bytes, which has a paid and a free version. As with the virus protection software, it comes in two parts, the software itself and the ongoing definitions (I don't know why it's named this; all I can say is that computer guys are typically not very good with languages. They communicate with each other in a kind of 'guy code' but often have trouble making sense to non-technicals). If you've been noodling around on the internet and your computer seems to be running slow or having trouble loading web pages, run your anti-malware program and clean the computer. It will delete cookies and temporary files and is a good way to improve the performance of your computer as well as take care of some nasties that may be residing on your hard drive. Trojans which can steal passwords and financial logins and information are cleaned by these programs. It used to be that just anti-virus was enough to keep your machine fairly safe but these days it is important to use a malware cleaner at least once a month, if not more.

Using a rolling bag damages your laptop. People don't believe this when I say it but every laptop that I've supported that's been regularly put in a rolling laptop bag gets damaged. The hard drive fails or some other component goes bad on them. It may not happen right away but the chances of having a hardware failure are greatly increased by bumping your laptop along in a rolling bag. Use a shoulder bag or backpack, it's much easier on the equipment. Or use the rolling bag but be sure to backup your data.

Defrag your hard drive every once in a while. Especially if you've had your computer for a while, and techs see many which have been around for years, defragging your hard drive will improve performance and reduce the load on the hard drive when opening programs and documents. When you open and close documents the computer doesn't always store the document back where it came from, but will use the closest available space. The items, when changed frequently, will become 'fragmented', which means that parts of it will be stored in various areas on the hard drive, making use of small pieces of available space to complete the whole document. The user is not aware of this because the computer fetches the document and re-assembles it as thought it was stored all in one piece. By defragging, you are telling the computer to go in and re-organize documents so that they are no longer fragmented. This process takes a long time, and all of your programs and documents must be closed, so choose a time when you don't need to use the computer and just let it run until complete. When you begin the defragger, it will show an analysis of the area that will be freed up by defragging. Sometimes the information the program gives you says it does not need to be defragged, but do it anyway, especially if it's been several months since your last defrag. It won't help to do it more often than necessary but it does help once every six months or so. Many computers have never been defragged and have been in use for several years, which means that defragging is way overdue.

Turn on Windows update. It is very important to keep Windows updated and the best way to accomplish this is to use the default settings in Windows, which will usually update every week, if new updates are available. I would not recommend daily updates as sometimes there are conflicts and flaws in the packages being deployed. When you are an 'update junkie', rushing out to get the latest update as soon as it's available, you become the guinea pig for Microsoft to do more testing on how the update works with your system. Once a week updates are normally sufficient, and once you set it up it will find and install the updates without your having to do anything else. Usually after updating your computer will automatically reboot for the installs to complete so be prepared for some extra time to login after these updates. If you turn your computer off at night it will perform the update as soon as you boot up and log on, which will slow your system and require a reboot first thing. It may be best to leave the computer on so that the update and reboot can be handled automatically. Then all you will need to do is log on for the rest of the install. Typically, Microsoft will push these out on a Wednesday so if you set your updates to install at 3:00 am, you'll be good to go first thing on Thursday.

Leave it on or turn it off? That's the question. It really doesn't matter that much any more. It used to be that hardware failure was a fairly common problem with computers and the most likely time to fail was on boot up. For that reason many people left the machines running in hopes of saving the hard drive or other components from the added stress of boot up. But these days hardware failure is much more rare, although hard disk drives are still susceptible, but not because of boot up, just wear and tear. So if you want to shut it down and boot up in the morning, go ahead. When working as a systems administrator I always shut my computer down when I left the office but it was more from a security aspect that anything else. Now that I am not in that role I typically leave my system running most of the time, with it set to go into sleep mode after about forty five minutes. With sleep and hibernate, the computer is essentially shut down as far as the electrical use is concerned. However, if you do prefer to leave your machine on, be sure to shut it down and boot up again once in a while to refresh the OS.

Hard and soft boots are different. Typically, a soft boot is just a restart of the machine, accomplished by choosing restart from the power or Start menu. A hard boot, sometimes called a cold boot means that the computer has been shut down and left turned off for at least a few minutes, long enough for any code that might be held in RAM to go into the bit bucket. This is the main difference between the two, that a soft boot will not erase the information loaded into RAM when the computer boots back up. The hard boot is often used as a means of clearing up operating system glitches and is the first thing to try before calling for technical support. I once had a co-worker who thought that pushing the button on the front of her desktop computer would turn it off, and was surprised when she came in the next morning and saw that it was still running. She assumed that the tech support staff (me, that is), had booted it up to do work during the night. Use the shut down command under the start button or if the computer is frozen, press and hold the power button for up to fifteen seconds until it shuts down.

Don't buy a gaming machine to use for as a business computer. There's a reason why businesses used Pentium processors and gamers use Athlons. Don't try to switch the two because the software made for both of these processors doesn't always work well with the opposite processor. Especially when running accounting software with database packages, go with the Pentium processor. I can promise that you won't regret it.

Scrub those disks! So many people use their computer for online banking, paying bills and purchasing over the internet that it has become extremely important to scrub the hard drive before getting rid of the computer, whether you're selling it or giving it away to a friend, or donating it to a non-profit or other good cause. If you aren't comfortable with scrubbing the disks, which involves using software packages that range in price from free, which are the least effective, to extremely expensive data erasing packages, have your local tech shop scrub it for you. There are different levels of scrubbing, from one pass of ones, which is the least effective, to patterns of ones and zeros produced by an algorithm which are extremely difficult to recover data from. Anything that says it meet the Department of Defense (DoD) requirements will be sufficient for personal use and for most business use. If in doubt there's always taking the hard drive out and taking the blow torch to it, but that means it will no longer be able to be used. Get a good scrubber or take it to your local computer shop and have them scrub and reformat the hard drive. Better safe than sorry.

Back up your data. Eventually, all hard drives will fail, at least until they no longer have moving parts. The best case scenario is that you replace your computer before the drive fails causing you to lose all of your data. Prior to the purchase you should have everything moved over to the new machine, or copied to a USB thumb drive or external hard drive. Having a system restore on the same hard drive will not help you when the drive fails. Always store copies of important documents, photos and music you wish to keep somewhere off of the computer itself. Important documents should be stored in a different location from the computer in case of fire, flood or other natural disaster. This is something that's easy to forget about until it happens to you. Recovering data from a failed hard drive is very expensive, usually in the several hundred dollars to over a thousand dollars for a medium size hard drive. If you're willing to pay the high price, most data is recoverable, but not always. A regular back up schedule is a good idea. There are also automatic off-site backups available to the home user which may be the best choice as these services have come down in price until they compete with the cost of a good external hard drive.

Beware the phishing scam. These are emails which look like real emails, asking you for confidential information after you click on a link in the email. They can come from your bank, LinkedIn, Facebook, even the FBI or the government. Because it is possible for the 'From' section of emails to be faked, it looks like it's a real request but don't be fooled. If you receive something like this go to your real account, NOT by clicking on the link provided, which always takes you to some other site (check the address bar at the top of the page), but by your usual login, and make sure everything is as it should be. I recently received one of these saying that my PayPal payment to someone I had never heard of had been sent. I clicked on the link but saw immediately that it wasn't PayPal at all. I closed that page before it could load fully, went to my PayPal account and found that no payment had been made to that person – it was a scam trying to get me to enter my PayPal password. I kept a check on the account over the next couple of days to make sure my password had not been hacked. I almost got caught though, so never click those links, go to your site directly.

Hacking your email account has become more and more prevalent. It used to be that viruses on your computer would automatically start sending out fake emails from your address book. These were usually embarrassing emails about Viagra or some other drug and they were actually coming from your email address even though you hadn't sent them personally. Now it's possible for those in the know to spoof, or hack your email address in the 'From' section of the email, without ever accessing your computer. What happens is you will experience a lot of bounces, which are return receipts for bad email addresses. Many people think that the sender has somehow accessed their email account, but it isn't necessary for them to spoof or hack your email. All they need is a valid address in the send field. The main difference in this case is that they are using their own addresses to send to, so most of the ones that bounce back will be to people you've never even heard of. The only thing to do in this case is to contact your email host provider and inform them of the problem. They will stop all email activity from the real IP address. It's still a good idea to go in and change your password and make sure your virus protection software is up to date. Using all of these tools together will usually stop the hacking. Don't let it go on for too long because if you do you run the risk of getting on the spam lists and spam filters, which will block legitimate emails from your address.

Clean out your mailbox. Having looked at thousands of email boxes over the years, and seen literally millions of emails, it is always the case that getting rid of old emails make mailboxes, and people, function better. There are many, many people who never delete anything in their Inbox which means that most of what they have in there is junk that they will never read. I knew one man who kept newsletters from a professional organization which he never read! Not a single one was opened yet he kept them in his Inbox, and then complained that he could never find the email he was looking for. I have also noticed that successful CEO's and top managers have almost nothing in their Inbox. They either delegate the item to someone else or take care of it, and then erase it or file it away for future reference. I always say that email is just like regular mail from the post office. You get rid of ninety percent of that mail and you should do the same with email. Deal with it and get it out of your Inbox. You will function better and your mailbox will function better. In the old days Outlook did have a limit on the size of the mailbox file, which took a long time and a lot of emails to fill up, but once it did, the file would corrupt and everything in it was lost. These days the limit is so large that very few would ever reach it, but take my advice and keep your Inbox as empty as you can. You won't regret it, I promise.

If in doubt, don't click. Recently I was called to a person's home to help her with her Internet Explorer, which had quit working properly. When I looked at the desktop the person opened up their browser and went to their home page, and immediately began clicking on whatever 'offer' was showing on the top of the Yahoo screen. It may have looked like a message from Internet Explorer but it was really an advertisement for some unnecessary program, a kind of malware that was being installed on the machine. By not taking the time to read the message and realize that it should be ignored, she had already installed dozens of add-ons to the Internet Explorer toolbar which meant that it would be extremely slow when trying to browse from page to page. And at that point the only way to get rid of all of them is to re-install the operating system, which erases everything on the computer. It's sometimes difficult to make users understand that they are their own worst enemies when it comes to using the Internet. Which leads to the subject of choosing a browser.

As mentioned earlier there are a number of **browsers which can be used for exploring the Internet**. A browser is simply a program for viewing html pages. Html is the code used to create web pages. The most popular browser by far is Internet Explorer, because it is installed as part of the operating system on all Windows based machines. Its icon is the baby blue lower case 'e' with the gold halo or orbit circling the upper left edge. It is usually found on the toolbar as well as the desktop of all Microsoft installed systems. While IE is the most popular web browser it is also the most prone to corruption and problems. There are a multitude of add-ons to the toolbar which clutter up the browser and while more convenient in a way, they are very likely to cause problems with the operation of the browser. Another thing that I believe can be a drawback to using Internet Explorer is that is does not use Google search by default, but uses its own version of a search engine called Bing. The results of the two search engines are vastly different, with Google being by far the better search engine. On Mac or Apple devices the built in browser is called Safari and it is at least much more stable than Internet Explorer. On Windows machines I always advise installing Mozilla Firefox or Google Chrome to use for internet browsing. The programs are slimmed down compared to Internet Explorer which means they load pages much more quickly and Chrome's visual display of pages recently visited is very helpful if you tend to check the same set of pages regularly. Both are free downloads from Google or Mozilla. Again, be careful not to automatically install added programs like anti-virus or other software packages during the installation.

Don't be trigger happy with the mouse. I've seen lots and lots of people who click first and ask questions later, which is always a bad combination on a computer. They seem to think that using the mouse is some kind of game and that the faster you can click the mouse the more points you receive. The opposite is true. There is no faster way to mess up your computer than to rapidly click through the program references while completing a task on your system. More problems are caused by people not taking the time to read, assuming that they already know what is going to be on the screen as soon as they see the box that pops up. The problem with that is that the boxes are standard and what's in them is not. Just because the box is the same size, shape and color as one you've seen before has nothing to do with the information inside it. Yes, it will always have a box to click on but the goal here is to read the information and choose the answer that causes the least harm. If there is no good answer, leave it alone or try closing it out or cancelling.

Save, save, save. I am always surprised at how often I see computers lock up while people are in the middle of a task and their work hasn't been saved. The worst example of this came when a co-worker had been working for hours on a huge spreadsheet and in the midst of it the computer froze and she lost most of her work. We were able to recover a small amount but not much. I am quite sure that she learned her lesson then, but it was a tough way to learn it. Whenever you are working on an important document of any kind, make a point to click on the 'save' icon after each paragraph or small section. With newer versions of MS Office the program will sometimes recover part of your work but I would never trust it entirely. Get in the habit of saving often and you won't regret it.

When you see the BSOD (blue screen of death), restart your computer but don't keep trying to boot it if you see more than one blue screen in a row. Very often a hard drive that will not boot is still readable by simply 'slaving' to a bootable hard drive, which can be done at your local computer shop for a reasonable fee. If you keep trying to start the computer you run the risk of the drive failing completely and at that point the only way to get the data off is to send it to a data recovery specialist, which will cost you as much as a new computer, usually, and sometimes more. Any clicking noises made by the hard drive warrant an immediate shut down as that's a sure sign that the drive is on its last leg.

Avoid adding programs to the system tray unless they are absolutely necessary. They system tray is right hand area of the bar at the bottom of the screen, next to the time. The worst offender in this category is weather. These programs cause your computer to run much more slowly than it would otherwise, because that program is always open, every time you turn your computer on, and is constantly communicating with the site behind the scenes. You can always have a weather web site as a favorite if you want to check the weather.

Internet access usually involves two pieces of equipment in addition to your computer. The first piece, which we will call the modem, is the box that the wires from the wall, either cable wire or phone wire, connect to. This box 'modulates' the signals so that your computer can read them. But in between the modem and your computer you should usually have what is called a router, sometimes a broadband router. Netgear, Linksys (now Cisco) and Belkin are some of the names you might recognize of these pieces of equipment. These allow you to connect more than one device to the modem and therefore to the Internet. They also provide another layer of protection between the modem and your computer and effectively hide your address from the outside world. Routers are notorious for going out on you due to power surges or lightning strikes. You usually only get a couple of years out of them. These days it's a good idea to get the wireless version which sometimes has small antennae on top, sometimes not. A router will cost anywhere from sixty to one hundred sixty dollars, depending on the type you get. If you stream movies over the internet, go with the higher priced versions. If all you do is send email and surf the web, the basic one will do. If you're handy with computer equipment you can pick up bargains on eBay but most of the equipment is used and may not have software to install it with. There's a way to get around that but if you don't know what you're doing, get a new one and the instructions and software in the box will guide you through the installation.

Geek Terms

Boot – start up the computer. There are two forms of this, soft and hard, with a soft boot being a restart, where the computer actually never shuts down, and a hard boot where the computer sits for a few minutes before powering up again. The latter can almost work miracles, sometimes.

BSOD – Blue Screen of Death, an ambiguous term that sometimes means death, sometimes means a hard drive is about to fail, and can mean a lot of other stuff too. Translation: try to shut down and reboot and if it happens again, take your computer, as quickly as you can, to your local computer shop.

Format – means to erase, to start over, to prepare for installation of software. Never do this unless you are absolutely certain you know what you are doing. Most computer users never do a format since it involves erasing the

About the author.

Mike Jessup has been working in the IT field for over fifteen years, supporting Windows based systems and users for business as well as in the home environment. He has made computer purchases for businesses and supported both users and equipment in various roles during his IT career. He studied networking and systems engineering at TechTrain, a partnership with Oglethorpe University in Atlanta and earned his certificate in 2001. A long-time resident of Atlanta, GA, he now lives in Birmingham, Alabama.

*To learn more about Windows computers, visit us online at **www.itlight.net**.*

operating system, and whatever else is on the disk. If in doubt, don't!

Killer App – refers to a program, or application, usually for a smartphone, but sometimes for computers as well.

Sleep – computers these days go into sleep mode, where all of the working components are shut off after a period of inactivity by the user. This is to conserve energy. You can change these settings in the display section of the Control Panel

Surf – means to browse the internet

Wipe – another term for format, with much greater 'geek effect'.

www.ingramcontent.com/pod-product-compliance
Lightning Source LLC
Chambersburg PA
CBHW061026050326
40689CB00012B/2709